Scandals

Filthy Loot

filthyloot.com

"Darkly comical, surreal, and at times, deeply touching."

— Sara B. (Artist)

"The tears of a clown clang against the floor like silver bullet casings. Speeding forward locked in battle with apparitions emerging from the afterburner, Alex Osman is in a league of his own."

— Gwen Hilton (author of *Sent to the Silkworm House* & *Where the Breastplate Meets the Blade*)

"I'll be honest – I jumped at the chance to blurb this book because it meant I didn't have to wait as long to read it. Alex Osman's work will do that to you. I needed another hit. No one else can find the absurdist wonder of dancing primates or toddlers graffitiing the KISS logo around their kindergarten.

Scandals – Alex Osman's strongest collection of writing so far – is full of cultural references – because the morning kids show entertainers, sitcom stars, the brand names of the day are the true landscape of the Americana that Osman chooses to mine and dissect with and within his work.

Osman is a genuine surrealist and understands the comedy, the horror, the pain, the immortal and yet constantly fleeting nature within everyday pop-culture. Something that adds a strength and depth to his multi-faceted body of work is that he also sees the beauty, the brief moments of truth and bliss amid the confusing blur of the whole mess of everything that makes up life. And we should be thankful that he does. Work this brilliant and evocative should be treated like the rare jewel that it is."

— Thomas Moore (author, *Forever*, *Alone*, & *Your Dreams*)

Scandals

Copyright © 2023 by Alex Osman

This book may not be reproduced in whole or in part, except for the inclusion of brief quotations in a review, without permission in writing from the author or publisher. No part of this publication may be reproduced, stored in or introduced into retrieval system, or transmitted, in any form, or by any means (electronic, mechanical, photocopying, recording, or otherwise), without prior permission of the publisher.

Requests for permission should be directed to filthylootpress@gmail.com

TALENTED PERVERTS™

Talented Perverts is a wholly owned subsidiary of Filthy Loot Enterprises.

Shane Jesse Christmass - Meth-dtf
Charlene Elsby - Letters to Jenny Just After She Died
Ira Rat - The Medication
Various - Little Birds (series)

PERPETUAL NOSTALGIA FOREVER®

Alex Osman lives in Texas with a former Moe Howard impersonator and a retired magician's assistant named Christina, who has a pet crawfish named Lardass. In pre-school, he won the award for "Pre-schooler With The Funniest Faces" and in 9th grade, the "Prankster Award".

Previous works include Problem Child (ExPat Press) and the self-released photozines Burgermeister and The Kennedy Vertigo.

the flaws, the open sores, the scandals, the car crashes

Love,
Alex Osman

Stage left: A pile of 8mm film reels containing thoughts, static images, reruns, failures, winners, and impossibilities soaked in lighter fluid and set on fire.

Center stage: Jayne Mansfield swimming in the absence of water.

Stage right: The child who dreamt it all.

TASTE OF HONEY

Inside a molar cavity
Reflected in a cold dental mirror
A small hive
Hanging from a nerve
Infant buzzing
Pulsating
One bee turned into a dozen
A dozen turned into a thousand
Crawling and flying
Out and away from the mouth
A string of vomit
Soon the walls were covered
It made everything look alive
And breathing
A loud drone
Like distorted tinnitus

NOTHING TO WRITE HOME ABOUT

"Don't walk around up there
 Don't even think about it
 That floor is haunted"
I never felt anything particular up here
But when I shifted my weight
As to balance on my left foot
It felt as though I were falling through the floor
Every now and then
A toilet would flush on its own
But nothing to write home about
They said someone threw themself
From a balcony
And you could still see her ghost
As it glides through a glass window
And makes a sudden drop
Apparently your heart would mimic
But as I said,
I experienced nothing
Nothing to write home about

THE TIMES OF SKIM MILK

This kid sold cans of soda by the bridge
Over the creek where his mom drowned kittens
Marissa sold illegal reptiles
Some guy was stabbed in a meth dispute
His brother got sick after drinking the water
And had to miss the homecoming game
Fingered this girl with carpal tunnel
And spray painted their initials on the concrete
Everything in that town changed
But the paint never faded

A recovering cokehead bought a Pepsi
And shotgunned the soda
In the middle of the bridge
Everyone says,
"He's changed"

DUPLEX

Shaved his ass raw as a cue ball
For a bathing mamacita
The compositions of a
Two-dollar roach
Screaming from a decrepit gramophone
He'd fade away into a clogged drain
If it weren't for sodium hydroxide
The soap made his urethra sting
It brought back
A memory from his childhood
He thought he had forgotten

I SHOULD HAVE SAID SOMETHING

When you're in my dreams
I oversleep

FUNERAL OUTFIT

SLAYER T-SHIRT
JEANS
BROKEN SUNGLASSES
DIRTY SNEAKERS
PEWTER PEKINGESE FIGURE
$5.75

FISH IN A BALLOON

I saw a pregnant girl
And wondered
Whether the baby
Would come into the world
As an invertebrate
Or a bastard

That belly could have been
A stolen pumpkin
For all I know

THE ROCKET'S RED GLARE

They came here looking for something
And they found it
And when they found it
It exploded like a hand grenade
They built a castle on this piece of land
And named it Black Betty
Their children would grow up in that castle
Their children would lose fingers in a
fireworks mishap
Their fingers would fill the empty gaps
When they hold hands
A look in those kids' exchanged glances
Would keep a secret

PUNK ASS

Teenage infrared
Happy days are here again
If the walls could talk
They'd say,
"¿Quién ha estado durmiendo debajo de la cama?"
The sound of a wind tunnel
Obfuscates his monologue
On hat tricks and colossal failures
Sister's in adjacent room
Sunbathing on the window sill
Her hair was washed in the bathroom sink

SUNDAY DRIVE

I'm working half-asleep overtime
To afford her favorite gun
Recoil in her embrace
And when we're old
And she comes across a thin green line
I unload the clip at the moon
Dead astronaut ornaments in memorial
Floating forever

UNTITLED4.WAV

They stole the liquor from a
bulimic football casualty
Tripped over dead trees
He punched a swollen spider's lights out
For dangling in her face
Those eight eyes
A fist in every eye

A wince in every sip
Hands were numb
Circulation under construction
Found themselves naked
In the house of a deer

SIDEKICKS

Elongated cadaver
Raised "Roman Cadillac"
Feelings isn't good
In the teeth
Anymore
Cavities isn't good
Anymore
Rack 'em up
Walk with a limp in a
Burnt down saloon
Where cavities are filled with
Opium ghosts
Opie, oh ghosts
Cadillac diaries torn to shreds

HE AIN'T HEAVY, HE'S MY BROTHER

Did Jacques Libbera know he was a star?

COMA EYE

A stray brick brought on the coma
The coma brought on a rape
He woke up 4 years later
A father of a daughter
It didn't matter
She was beautiful
She had his eyes
Those coma eyes

The sensation of a
Phantom catheter
Caused sleepless nights
In a house of larvae
And varve clay

A PERFECT MONTH FOR CHRONIC WASTING DISEASE

A subcutaneous love affair
Terrified of each other
Despite the romance
Bad weather for birds came
They both died natural in a
Sleeping bag cocoon
Mistaken for kiviak

IT HAPPENS EVERY TEN YEARS

Kick off your shoes
Let's become persona non grata
And crawl under the porch to die
Like decade dogs

JESUS LOUISE-US

His feet were crossed
No they weren't
Yeah they were
Right over left?
Or left over right?
Couldn't have been much
Leftover
Crows love a dead man

TURKEY NECK

The tireless nurse
Saved her bandages
For her vile husband
The convoy bastard
Trademark Adderall facial scabs
Saliva bullets in his language
The tireless nurse
Collected small screws
Her vile husband's turkey was
Embedded on Thanksgiving

UNCLE GARY'S IN PRISON AGAIN

A case of beer
Turned into
A case of vehicular manslaughter

NATIONAL DAY OF LAUGHTER

On the day I was born
The doctor laughed
And anytime I went in
For a routine checkup
He would just laugh
He took it to his grave
They played videos at his funeral
Multi-screen laughter
A cramped floral room
Of crying and laughing
Laughing, choking, laughing
It keeps getting funnier and funnier

I love you, James'"

Jughead flew her to the moon and back
Maxine barked at them
They laid nude in a red room
Faces lit by the TV
Smoke poured in from the windows
They fell asleep

most vulnerable
Wants to keep a magnifying glass on you
'Til the sun comes and burns you away
Just black dust on a hill
Maxine was always there

Jughead liked hanging out with prostitutes
He showed them his shopping carts
He liked to ask them,
"Have you ever been up on the roof of a skyscraper
Looked down on the street below
And swear you could fly?"

Tay replied,
"Even if I couldn't
If I fell and died
My soul would fly
My soul would fly and write love letters
In after-death chemtrails
In the deepest blues of the sky
I'd write,
'I love you, mom',
'I miss you, honey'"
My two year-old James
I'd write,
'Mommy's okay
Nobody can hurt me
And nobody will ever hurt you

CONEHEADS 2

He's the last conehead on earth
When he came to this planet
Everyone called him Jughead
He's not an idiot
He just don't read too good
If you tell him a joke on Monday
He won't get it until Friday
Coneheads eat 3 meals a day
Celebrate birthdays
Smoke cigarettes
Stuff like that
Not much different at all

Ain't nothing been the same since his brother died
in that car wreck
Ain't shit been the same
Neck snapped
Legs broken
No seatbelt
Not meant to live long
He was a heretic
There won't be a funeral held for him

Jughead took Maxine
She was his brother's love
A good watch dog
Everybody wants a look inside when you're

L.T. THE LEPRECHAUN OF TEXAS

"Probably has diabetes
You can smell it on him
People with diabetes,
They got a certain smell to them
Yeah, he's a diabetic, alright"
–my coworker with the fake eye

Her wig fell off on a moped ride
In the middle of a street takeover
Cars and trucks leaving circles and smoke
Kids were hanging out in trees
Someone got hit by a red Impala
Cops arresting people left and right
You could see pieces of her wig on the sidewalk

SCENT OF EASTER

Mom covered our furniture in plastic
The couch was always uncomfortable
When our house caught fire
It smelled funny
The smell made me sick
Today's Easter
Eggs all the same shade of blue
She doesn't hide the baskets anymore

BUCKWHEAT

My daughter could make frogs dance
By whistling Eddie Cantor
Befriended a former concubine
And showed her the lifeboat
One foot in the grave
One foot in the boat
The fat frog mausoleum
Stood by the pier

The black girl with the missing teeth
The one with the slanted truck
She was glazing the ham
Made the ham limbo
She liked to dance with pigs
And frogs
And pigs and frogs

WHEN BOYS TELEPHONE GIRLS

They watch like peeping toms
We're growing roots in my bed
Epileptics in shock
It's all so temporary
I wish it wasn't
A voyeuristic paranoid can't help but
Jack off in a fugue state
In the backseat of a
Tinted window deathtrap
Adam & Eve in the scope of an unloaded rifle

FOR THE LOVE OF TAR

I saw a man so desperate
He lit a cigarette with a magnifying glass
On a sunny day
His eyes were bigger than his lungs

WON'T GET FOOLED AGAIN

Fool me once
I'll kill you

DOCTOR'S NOTE

She loves like a cannonball
Looks like a loaded rifle
Everytime she comes around
She's like a
Runaway symptom
Explode choking, grabbed lethargy
Lipstick in the maternity ward
Sticks around for
Weekly soap enema
She had come to enjoy the burn
She gave her mother
Herpes simplex

I LOVE SHIRLEY

Choke on the pistol
Massage the afterglow
Miss Mayberry's oven self-death
She says something smells peculiar
You say return to sender
And grow a third arm bent backwards
Gravity loaded in her pistol
Made sure to capsize the county

Oh, and here comes Barney Fife
Drowning in pneumonia brine
Fake meat on the highway
Fake meat in the precinct
Fake meat growing
Bent backwards

WHISPERS FROM THE EXO-APPARITION

I dreamt I was a cricket
With a disgusting human face
Consistency and color of
Burnt rotisserie skin
I was beaten with a stick by a cherub
And tossed into hectic traffic
I watched black blood flow
From my tightly closed mouth
Eyes twitched like billiard failures
Bladder emptied red clouds
"How does it feel?
 How does it feel, kid?
 You feel the cold numbness in your legs?
 You feel scared?
 You feel the magnification?
 Asphalt glue?
 The texture of your own blood
 Bile
 Vomit
 Stomach acid
 Half-digested this and that
 Pouring over your isosceles chin?
 Let's see how it fucking feels."
Whispers from the exo-apparition

It felt great

BLANKS

Those living within the confines
Of skin tags and cuticles and cavities
Self-obsessed serial blamers
Fish in the pockets of their jeans
To throw into adjacent trails
Masking and distracting the scent of
Their own shit
A television fantasy
[deleted scene]
[deleted scene]
[deleted scene]

"Let me tell you something about
'We the people'
We the people who ain't shit"

The blue parka junkie
Investigated the lobby trash cans
Full of the previous night's
Mistakes and regrets
"Found a Fiver"
The woman who stabbed the horse
Covered head to toe in
Stallion blood
Brightened her complexion
"It's like getting
Head in a haunted house
It's not all so tragic"

IT'S NOT ALL SO TRAGIC

I saw an albino named OJ order a sausage pizza
The same I night I saw a woman sneak around
a stable
To stab and kill a horse
The same week I saw a junkie in a blue parka
Shoot up outside the crab shack
He was on the nod and
Having trouble pulling down his sleeve
Shoes on my feet are getting old
Soles slipping out like dirty tongues
OJ's shoes were brand new
Not a scuff
Like a clean freak

The woman who stabbed the horse
Covered head to toe in
Stallion blood
She stood sober in the motel lobby
Asking questions
Vacancy?
Outdated cameras?
Perverted surveillance?
Careless police uniforms on the way
She asked,
"What ever happened to
'We the people'?"
OJ waded in a pool of laughter

100 PROOF

On the day Jim Varney died
I was 4 months away from
Graduating kindergarten
Where I told a classmate to
Go to Hell
Wrote the KISS logo on the walls
Pretended to sleep at assemblies
So the teacher's assistant with the big tits would
Pick me up and carry me
Back to class
Where Cody threatened to stab a crying classmate
With a *Toy Story* pencil

I brought a lighter to school
So we could smoke the cigarette we found
Near the playground
Jim Varney was a chain smoker
He died of lung cancer at age 50

On the day Jim Varney died
I was 4 going on 5
5x10
50
50x2
100 proof

DILUTED SOLUTION FOR CRYBABIES

Dreams of starlets with blue LED-lit uzis
Glow-in-the-dark headstones for
Claustrophobic troubled kids
Sunday paper in the thorax
Bags are lined with synthetic dirt
A latex skyscraper casts a jaded shadow
Another dead sex symbol

TRIPLE DIGIT

My broken air conditioning unit
Is enough to drive any otherwise sane individual
Up a fucking wall
If I had a dollar for every
Irate hitchhiker
I'd have enough money
To buy stocks in the company that produces
Earthquakes in California

CLONE BASEBALL

Umbilical imbecile
Umbrella for the umpire
The empire of the imitator
A house of mirrors
Who's who?
500 reflected umbilical hernias
A real idiot
Wipe that shit-eating grin off your face
Play ball in the rain
Catch pneumonia in a gifted mitt
Wipe those droplets off your doppelgangers
Your cord resembles a rejected tourniquet

BADA-BING BADA-BOOM

My role in life is the jester
Class clown
Entertainer
Vaudeville act
But I'm closing the curtains on this life
I'll be nude at my funeral
With pallbearers on fire
The show is over

A SOUNDPROOF COFFIN

I don't want to die a legend, because then
I'll never die
When I'm dead, I'm dead
Eradicated like a crippling virus
I just want some quiet

BULL DOSE

Brutus Beefcake stabbed Cesar Romero
Swimming in the Atlantic with the remains
of Jim Jones
Jimmy Carter avoided cruise ships
A tired goat missionary
Toothy matador given a California smile
Ribs shattered by the weight of his arrogance
Black blood stained a false gilded jacket

He looked like Al Lewis playing the saxophone

DRAWER OF USED PENCIL ERASERS

Crystallized
And on display
Where lepers walk in patterns
But it don't mean anything

A crutch that's full of splinters
Covered in insect clay
Flying off the porch
In threes

BRASS CRAWFISH

I was the killer
Killed that son of a bitch
Killed him real good
Me and him
Found 500 pounds
Of brass crawfish
In the stomach of Buddy Holly

Buddy Holly was a reject
Buddy Holly was a star
Buddy Holly had a gun
Buddy Holly was a smartass
Buddy Holly was a mother to crustaceans
He was a host

ANTIHISTAMINE

It's not what you think
It's not what it seems
Don't pick the scabs
Don't scratch the itch
Just wish it away
Leave a mark
They multiply
Open sores, surface wounds
Causing infection
Watch it spread
Arms covered in red lines
Face covered
Shades of gray
Deflation
Lined in dirt

JOB

Interests were limited
Paychecks went straight to his veins
Most were already too abused to accommodate
The needle
He nodded off in the balcony at a matinee of
Jesus Christ Superstar
Sweet emotion
Infinite orgasm
Sucking the tit of Mother Mary
Cured his ills
Ending the night in the handbag
Of a whore

CHICKEN SHIT CALAMITY

I could stay awake and watch her
Slaughter chickens all day
Spare bedroom splattered in white shit
She took off her rings to keep them clean
She never removed her wedding ring
A disastrous marriage
Them bodies sure did dance when their heads
were removed

MORPHINE NIGHTS

Sometimes I miss the respiratory depression
And the thrill that I could die in my sleep
I felt good
And it wasn't until I jolted
Gasping for oxygen
That I felt bad again

CURE FOR LAUGHING RABBITS

He said his chair's too hard
Molasses was the cure
Haunted by rabbits twice his size
He barked like a dog, until he laughed
He laughed like a dog
He ran like a dog
He spit at the ceiling

And when his brother blew into his wife's cunt
He saw an angel fly out her mouth

CARBON MONOXIDE

Slip and fall and crack my head
Spilling out memories of Amish girls
I can't remember her love
But I remember her drugs

Cupid bought a double-barrel

A bear attack left me speechless
Ribs are broken, guts are planted
In the ground next to a soaking tent
My eyes are black and white
My arms are open wide
I'm breathing my baby's carbon monoxide
Bulging penis in my pants
Dressed in my funeral best
Mortician gave me a crooked smile
My brother's high on acid
Everyone says I look like Peewee Herman
Nobody mentions my name

STOMACH FULL OF NEEDLES

I hang in a room
I float
The ceiling is the floor
My head is revolving
I eat from your hand
Fragments of chalk
Smoke in your hair
You're fire

One more pill split for two
But it won't be the last

GRANDMA AND GRANDPA

Unsolved Mysteries
Cops
America's Most Wanted
Lottery numbers
Jerry Springer
Marlboro golds
Skoal long cut
<u>Playboy</u> magazines
12 gauge shotguns
Asthma inhalers
Old wigs
Parakeets
Pekingese
Star Trek
Late night porno flicks
Crossword puzzles
Vicodin
Prednisone
Tramadol
Viagra
Liquid Morphine
Paper airplanes
Arthritis
Above-ground swimming pools

MY INSURANCE IS A GREASY GUN

Your sickness won't come between us
They call me The Doctor
It's not a day job
Not some fantasy
This is fucking real life
I slither through you
Soak it up like a sponge

You're cured
I'm cured

My insurance is a greasy gun
Come with me

EL MONTEREY

Stick your head in a microwave
Give yourself a tan
This is your direction

Your brain is foil
Mustard on my muscle
PHD in Dollar Tree
I know everything there is to know about
trash meals

One minute is all it takes

VOLANTE

I used to stare into the clouds
I used to have sex with the Harmon sisters when
we were 8 years old
Richie started wearing his dead father's
sunglasses after he saw *Terminator 2*
He brought a hunting knife to school and dropped
it on the playground
Abby took it home with her and killed her dog
Me and Grant once looked up her skirt while we
ate licorice under the lunch table
I used to ride sun-faded dirt bikes
My mother would get nosebleeds
Her sister broke a lava lamp on the sidewalk when
they were young
She thought the lava would take out the whole
neighborhood
Their neighbor dated a guy who stocked vending
machines
He paid for dates with stolen quarters
He went to jail for a meth bust in 1997
The lab almost took out my friend Jacob's trailer
While they were in Disney World for his sister's
Make-A-Wish vacation

All those familiar faces come back to haunt me
again

WE NEVER GREW UP TO BE COWBOYS

I see bodies
I see bodies float face down
Face down in an above-ground swimming pool
And I watch the scarecrows grow wings
Fucking in fields
Fucking in the streets
Where needle fiends grow up to be cowboys

To feel safe in the belly of a whale
I see gold teeth
Gnawing and crushing the larynx
Stained brown
I see gold teeth stained brown

I'm fucking sick of paying the piper
Floating and stuck on the ceiling
Where I'll age 5 years in 5 hours
And my crooked soul
Seeps out from my fucking dick
And I just don't give a single shit about anything

Scarecrows in flight
Come to take me away
It's such a fucking shame
We never grew up to be cowboys

GOLD TOOTH IN A KNUCKLE SANDWICH

Look at this motherfucker
Looking like a cocaine dealer on *Starsky & Hutch*
Looking like a hitman on the *Love Boat*
Looking like he pistol whipped Mr. Drummond
and asked for $10M dollars and a toothpick
Looking like he's on his way to get his dick
sucked on *Gilligan's Island*
Looking like he sucker punched *ALF* and shipped
his ass off to Coney Island in an Amazon box
Looking like he'd wave a golden 9mm in a
leprechaun's face
Looking like he eats Corn Flakes with no
added sugar
Looking like he wipes his ass with Fonzi's
leather jacket
Looking like his wife runs a laundromat that's a
front for a money laundering scheme
Looking like he smokes crack rocks with Tattoo
on *Fantasy Island*
Looking like he'll one day be shot dead on a
yacht named the S.S. Punky Brewster

THE MECHANICS OF PARASITIC MIMICRY

Irritable spectators brawl like pinball
Recycling oxygen from lung implants
The Surgeon General retired his Sunday shackles
for a right-eye shiner

Ants! Ants! Ants!

Ants live in the esophagus
He sugarcoats the unfortunate with glucose lies
Antennas transmit pheromones to the fiending
spectators

A YOUNG PERSON'S GUIDE TO DROWNING

This is the site where he drowned
Where geriatric paranoia manifested
Where childhood boogeymen lurked under rafts
Divers' capillaries were jade
Underwater barber shop quartet members sang
with algae in follicles
Where the whites of eyes were made known
Distance grew an extra inch
Forgotten fishing hooks punctured
unsuspecting legs
Teenage lust ran rampant
Where his lungs caught fire
Grisly mono-endings were disposed
Where revival attempts were made by an assumed
TV infatuation

This is the site where he drowned

CHOLAME

I can't help but rubberneck
On the day of the amputation
Dual rear wheels generating friction
Second-degree asphalt scarring
Reminiscent of an infant exaggeration
Hyphema like pre-slaughter cattle
Chain-link skin graft souvenirs
Visions of Camelot on cortex security tape
Narcosis fuelled the engine of a James Dean
dream

FISTFUL OF FARMAPRAM

"Better to have a drug and not need it
Than to need a drug and not have it"
The name Leadbelly left her confused
Blanket of skin
The comfort of the flesh
The natural fear of decay of the flesh
Excitement
A tension headache nearly caused
An accident
Lock jaw kept her quiet
While she waited for metal
And flesh
To collide
And create the new Leadbelly
She hoped to descend from the glove
compartment
And live forever
Just to watch everyone she loved
die

THIS TRAILER WILL COLLAPSE AND FERTILIZE THE EARTH

Passed on a college degree
This whole time I wanted a dancing primate
I've never seen three crooked cops watching those late night talk shows
Put it in reverse, you just want to be loved
Put it in neutral, a tragic stilt charade
I don't give a shit
Exhaust fumes remain nostalgic
Microwave dinners melting in a vacuum
Lawn gnomes don't practice basic hygiene
Hand-me-down knick knacks from porno geeks
A chicken beheaded
A chicken unbreaded
That cartilage will come back in style
Neighbor presented the blade
9 year old anger management case
The eyes of Rick Ramirez
Riding a chicken through the eye of a tornado
Grinding it's organs to make his final meal
I was the organ grinder on the trampoline
performing with a dancing primate

"THIS TRAILER WILL COLLAPSE AND FERTILIZE THE EARTH" appeared in *MAXIMUS* 2.

"CHOLAME", "A YOUNG PERSON'S GUIDE TO DROWNING", and "THE MECHANICS OF PARASITIC MIMICRY" appeared in *BRUISER*.

"GOLD TOOTH IN A KNUCKLE SANDWICH", "IT'S NOT ALL SO TRAGIC", and "THE TIMES OF SKIM MILK" appeared in *Expat Press*.

"BULL DOSE", "DILUTED SOLUTION FOR CRYBABIES", "CURE FOR LAUGHING RABBITS", "I LOVE SHIRLEY", "SCENT OF EASTER", and "A PERFECT MONTH FOR CHRONIC WASTING DISEASE" appeared in *DON'T SUBMIT!*

www.ingramcontent.com/pod-product-compliance
Lightning Source LLC
LaVergne TN
LVHW092057060526
838201LV00047B/1442